Will My Haircut Hurt?

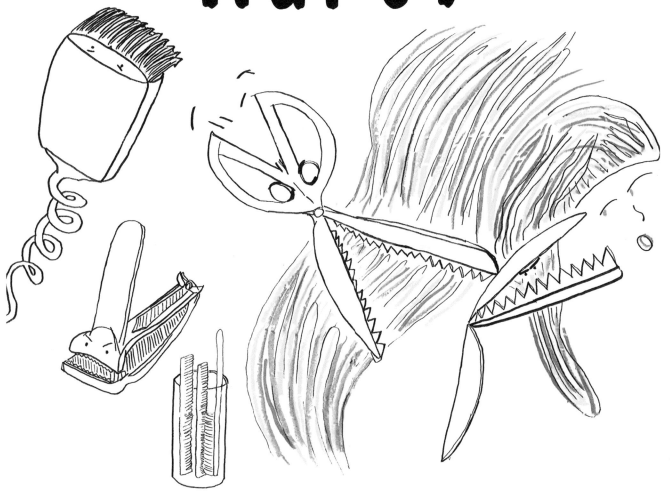

By Martha Goldner

To order additional copies of this book, contact:
Xlibris
844-714-8691
www.Xlibris.com
Orders@Xlibris.com

ISBN: Softcover   979-8-3694-2045-4
       Hardcover   979-8-3694-2044-7
       EBook   979-8-3694-2043-0

Print information available on the last page

Rev. date: 04/25/2024

This book belongs to:

_____

Dedicated to all children of neglectful, abusive parents. These children never learn the value of self-care.

Martha Goldner

Mom says I need a haircut. I don't want one.
I'm afraid it will hurt.

Will my haircut need Band-Aids?

Will they be big?

Pulling bandages off of cuts feels prickly.

I don't want a haircut.

Scissors scare me.

I had to go to the hospital.

Will blood come out of my hair when it is cut?

Will my hair need stitches?

I don't want a haircut.

Hairdressers use clippers sometimes.

Maybe a haircut will feel like having my nails clipped.

Snip. (click)   Snip (click)   Snip (click)

Some clippers are dull.

Instead of cutting, they bend or break things part of the way.

Will that happen when I get my haircut?

"Yeow!"

I don't want a haircut.

My dad has an electric razor that cuts hair just like the barber's.

It goes *buzzzzzz, buzzzzzz,* like bumblebees.

Once, I was stung by a bee on my elbow.

I cried.

Mom put pink calamine lotion on it.

Will my haircut feel like bumblebee stings all over my head?

Will my hair need pink calamine lotion after it is cut? I don't want my hair cut.

My friend had a "boo-boo bruise."

The scratch swelled and turned black and blue.

After a cut, will my hair swell and turn black and blue, too, like my friend's boo-boo bruise?

I don't want my hair cut.

Not too long ago, my aunt Weezy saw a hair hanging in my face.

She said, "You need a haircut," and tugged and pulled the hair so hard—

"Ouch!"

It came out!

Will my haircut feel like Aunt Weezy tugging and pulling?

I don't want my hair cut.

"*What will you do instead?*" Mom asks.

"I can let it grow longer."

"But then people may not recognize you."

"I will pull it back and hide my long hair under a hat."

"It is not always good manners to wear a hat indoors."

"You could buy me a wig."

"Most wigs are made for grown-ups. It may not fit."

"Uncle Bill never has to get a haircut."

"Neither does Great-Aunt Sally in the nursing home."

"I wish I didn't have any hair."

"I do not think you would like to be bald."

"I am afraid to get my hair cut! I am going to let it grow and grow and grow forever!"

"But then how will I find your lips when I want to give you a kiss?"

"Hmmmmmm. The chairs are high and look fun to sit in."

"The stylists seem friendly ..."

"No one here is crying or screaming ..."

"In that case, can I have all my hairs cut, not just one?"

"Of course."

The date of my first haircut was:

_____